THE ANTI INFLAMMATORY MEDITERRANEAN DIET COOKBOOK

1500 Days of Nourishing and Tasty Gluten-Free Recipes to Help Reduce Inflammation and Boost Wellness

CHRISTIE R. WILSON

Table of Contents

Introduction

Amidst the rolling hills of Santorini, a sun-kissed island in the heart of the Mediterranean, a story of transformation begins. Picture Sophia, a young woman seeking solace from the storms of chronic inflammation. In the pages of this cookbook, she discovers more than recipes; she uncovers a pathway to vitality. From the first sizzle of olive oil to the aroma of basil, Sophia not only crafts delectable dishes but also sews the seeds of wellness. Her pains begin to wane, and her energy returns like a long-lost friend.

In a world where the chaos of modern life often overshadows our well-being, a culinary oasis emerges—

The Anti-Inflammatory Mediterranean Diet Cookbook. Here, amidst the timeless allure of Mediterranean flavors, we embark on a transformative expedition towards a healthier, more vibrant self.

As the sun sets over azure waters and cobblestone streets, this cookbook becomes your compass, guiding you through the intricate tapestry of nourishment and wellness. Our voyage is fueled by the harmonious synergy of deliciousness and health, where every recipe is a testament to the remarkable power of food as medicine.

Step into this world of fresh produce, aromatic herbs, and nourishing grains, where vibrant colors and intricate flavors paint a picture of well-being. From earthy salads to succulent seafood, from morning awakenings to evening comforts, we journey together through pages rich with stories of healing, resilience, and renewal.

This cookbook isn't just about meals; it's about rewriting narratives. It's about savoring each bite with the knowledge that healing can be delicious. As you venture forth, remember: every dish is an embrace, every recipe a story of hope. Let these recipes be your anchors, grounding you in the wisdom of centuries and the science of today. As you embrace this culinary adventure, remember: each dish is an ode to your vitality, and each bite is a step towards a life lived fully and joyfully.

Join us as we celebrate the union of flavor and health, in kitchens worldwide, one plate at a time.

Chapter 1
The Basics of Anti-Inflammatory Mediterranean Diet

At the crossroads of health and gastronomy lies the Anti-Inflammatory Mediterranean Diet—a transformative approach to nourishment that transcends mere sustenance. This dietary philosophy marries the principles of the traditional Mediterranean diet with the modern understanding of inflammation's impact on our bodies.

Inflammation, a natural defense mechanism, can spiral into chronic health issues if left unchecked. The Anti-Inflammatory Mediterranean Diet acts as a soothing balm, harnessing the power of wholesome, nutrient-dense foods to quell inflammation's flames.

This section dives into the intricacies of inflammation, distinguishing between acute and chronic states while shedding light on the pro-inflammatory and anti-inflammatory foods that shape our well-being. By cultivating an awareness of what we put on our plates, we empower ourselves to take control of our health.

Delving deeper, we uncover the Mediterranean Diet's pillars—abundant fruits and vegetables, lean proteins, healthy fats, whole grains, and an array of herbs and spices. This balanced culinary symphony is more than just a collection of ingredients; it's a harmonious orchestra, playing in sync with our bodies' rhythms.

Through engaging explanations and practical guidelines, we demystify the mechanics of this diet. From understanding the role of antioxidants to embracing the magic of olive oil, these insights illuminate the path toward a life marked by vitality and well-being. As you embark on this journey, remember that each mindful choice in the kitchen brings you closer to a healthier, more vibrant you.

Demystifying Inflammation: Your Path to Healing

Inflammation, often regarded as the body's response to injury or infection, is a complex physiological process that wields both protective and destructive powers. This chapter delves into the nuanced world of inflammation, unraveling its dual nature and its pivotal role in our health.

From acute inflammation's role in wound healing to the insidious undercurrent of chronic inflammation in various diseases, we uncover the spectrum of this biological response. By understanding the triggers and mechanisms that propel inflammation, we empower ourselves to adopt proactive measures.

Guided by scientific insights, we explore the delicate balance between pro-inflammatory and anti-inflammatory foods. Delving into the former, we decipher the detrimental effects of processed sugars, refined oils, and excessive saturated fats. Conversely, we celebrate the latter, highlighting the heroes of inflammation reduction—richly colored fruits, omega-3 fatty acids, and an array of antioxidants.

As we navigate this exploration, remember that knowledge is the beacon guiding us toward sound dietary choices. The journey to healing and wellness begins with appreciating the body's wisdom and nurturing it with foods that foster vitality.

Exploring Chronic vs. Acute Inflammation

In the intricate landscape of human biology, inflammation emerges as a multifaceted phenomenon with distinct faces—acute and chronic. Acute inflammation, akin to a rapid-response team, arises in response to immediate threats like infections and injuries. This transient process involves immune cells rushing to the affected area, orchestrating a defense mechanism that promotes healing.

On the other hand, chronic inflammation embodies a more subtle, sustained narrative. Unlike its acute counterpart, chronic inflammation is not a discrete event but an underlying condition with systemic repercussions. It's associated with conditions ranging from cardiovascular diseases and diabetes to autoimmune disorders and even some cancers.

This exploration delves into the dynamic contrast between these two forms of inflammation. Acute inflammation, the body's defender, is celebrated for its promptness and precision. In contrast, chronic inflammation's hidden impact unfolds over time, quietly contributing to the development and progression of various ailments.

Understanding this duality is crucial in the pursuit of holistic well-being. Armed with this knowledge, we can tailor our dietary choices to mitigate the risk of chronic inflammation, embracing a menu rich in antioxidants, omega-3 fatty acids, and phytochemicals—key allies in the fight against sustained inflammation's potential havoc.

As we navigate the delicate balance between these twin aspects, let us approach our diets and lifestyles with awareness, crafting a symphony of choices that harmonize with the body's innate rhythms and support enduring health.

Foods That Fuel Inflammation: The Culprits

These culprits stand out as contributors to inflammation, potentially leading to various health challenges.

Refined Sugars: Sugary treats and beverages can trigger spikes in blood sugar levels, prompting the body's inflammatory response. Processed sugars found in many packaged foods can contribute to chronic inflammation over time.

Trans Fats: Often hidden in processed and fried foods, trans fats promote inflammation and raise the risk of heart disease. They interfere with cell function and promote the release of inflammatory chemicals.

Processed Carbohydrates: Foods made with refined flour and devoid of fiber, such as white bread and sugary cereals, can cause rapid spikes in blood sugar, leading to an inflammatory response.

Omega-6 Fatty Acids: Found in vegetable oils like corn, soybean, and sunflower oil, excessive omega-6 fatty acid consumption can disrupt the balance of omega-3 to omega-6 ratios, promoting inflammation.

High in saturated fats and compounds formed during cooking, these meats can trigger inflammation and are associated with an increased risk of chronic diseases.

Alcohol: Excessive alcohol intake can impair gut health, leading to increased gut permeability and the release of pro-inflammatory molecules into the bloodstream.

Artificial Additives: Artificial additives, such as certain food colorings and preservatives, can trigger inflammatory responses in some individuals.

Awareness of these culprits empowers us to make conscious dietary choices. While moderation is key, opting for whole, nutrient-dense foods, rich in antioxidants and healthy fats, can help counteract the inflammatory effects of these foods.

Foods That Fight Inflammation: The Heroes

These heroes possess the remarkable ability to quell inflammation and nurture our bodies toward optimal vitality.

Fruits and Berries: Bursting with antioxidants, vitamins, and fiber, fruits like berries, cherries, and citrus fruits combat inflammation by neutralizing harmful free radicals.

Leafy Greens: Kale, spinach, and other leafy greens are rich in vitamins, minerals, and antioxidants that help regulate inflammation and support immune function.

Fatty Fish: Omega-3 fatty acids found in salmon, mackerel, and sardines possess anti-inflammatory properties that can alleviate chronic inflammation and reduce the risk of chronic diseases.

Nuts and Seeds: Walnuts, flaxseeds, and chia seeds provide a dose of healthy fats, fiber, and antioxidants that aid in dampening inflammatory responses.

Olive Oil: Extra virgin olive oil is abundant in monounsaturated fats and polyphenols, which work together to mitigate inflammation and promote heart health.

Turmeric and Ginger: These potent spices contain curcumin and gingerol, compounds known for their anti-inflammatory effects, aiding in the reduction of chronic inflammation.

Whole Grains: Rich in fiber and nutrients, whole grains like quinoa, brown rice, and oats have been linked to reduced inflammation and improved overall health.

Legumes: Beans, lentils, and chickpeas offer a blend of protein, fiber, and antioxidants that can help curb inflammation and stabilize blood sugar.

Yogurt and Fermented Foods: Probiotics found in yogurt and fermented foods support gut health, influencing the body's inflammatory response positively.

Green Tea: Packed with polyphenols and antioxidants, green tea has been associated with decreased inflammation and potential protection against chronic diseases.

Including these heroes in your diet can foster a harmonious relationship between food and health, empowering you to proactively combat inflammation and embrace a life of vitality and well-being.

Unveiling the Mediterranean Diet's Core Principles

At the heart of the Mediterranean Diet lie principles that mirror the rich cultural heritage and vibrant landscapes of the Mediterranean region. This dietary approach isn't just about what's on the plate; it's a holistic lifestyle that fosters wellness, longevity and a profound connection to food and community. The Mediterranean Diet, therefore, transcends mere nutrition; it's a philosophy that aligns with the rhythms of nature and the pleasures of life.

Abundant Plant Foods: Embrace the colorful bounty of vegetables, fruits, legumes, and whole grains. These nutrient-dense foods provide vitamins, minerals, fiber, and antioxidants that support overall health.

Healthy Fats: Prioritize monounsaturated fats, as found in olive oil, nuts, and seeds. These fats protect the heart, regulate cholesterol levels, and contribute to a feeling of satiety.

Lean Proteins: Fish and poultry are preferred sources of protein, with red meat consumed in moderation. Fish, rich in omega-3 fatty acids, serves as a cornerstone for heart health.

Herbs and Spices: Embrace the aromatic allure of herbs and spices like basil, oregano, garlic, and turmeric. These flavor enhancers elevate meals while contributing to health benefits.

Moderate Dairy: Incorporate dairy in the form of yogurt and cheese, which offer probiotics and calcium. Choose lean options and consume in moderation.

Wine in Moderation: If you consume alcohol, opt for red wine in moderation, enjoying its potential heart-protective properties and cultural significance.

Physical Activity: The Mediterranean lifestyle emphasizes regular physical activity, be it walking, cycling, or engaging in outdoor pursuits.

Social Interaction: Meals are shared experiences, fostering a sense of community and connection. Engage in leisurely meals with family and friends.

Mindful Eating: Savor each bite, eating slowly and being attuned to hunger and fullness cues.

Seasonal and Local: Prioritize fresh, local, and seasonal ingredients, celebrating the flavors of the region and reducing environmental impact.

The Science Behind the Mediterranean Diet's Anti-Inflammatory Benefits

Research has illuminated how this diet's composition and components work in concert to soothe the flames of chronic inflammation, a precursor to various health concerns.

Omega-3 Fatty Acids: Abundant in fatty fish like salmon and sardines, omega-3 fatty acids are essential players in taming inflammation. These healthy fats curb the production of pro-inflammatory molecules, promoting a balanced immune response.

Antioxidants: The Mediterranean Diet overflows with antioxidant-rich foods such as colorful fruits, vegetables, and herbs. These antioxidants neutralize free radicals, the culprits behind inflammation and oxidative stress.

Monounsaturated Fats: Extra virgin olive oil, a cornerstone of the diet, boasts monounsaturated fats that not only support heart health but also exhibit anti-inflammatory effects by reducing levels of inflammatory markers.

Phytochemicals: Garlic, onions, and an array of aromatic herbs aren't just flavor enhancers; they contain bioactive compounds that mitigate inflammation, providing a natural defense against chronic disease.

Whole Grains and Fiber: Whole grains and legumes, staples of the Mediterranean Diet, are packed with fiber. This dietary fiber promotes gut health, influencing the gut microbiota in ways that curb inflammation.

Reduced Refined Sugars: By reducing the intake of refined sugars and processed foods, the Mediterranean Diet minimizes the triggers for inflammation, stabilizing blood sugar levels and promoting overall health.

Gut Health: Emerging science underscores the intimate connection between gut health and inflammation. The Mediterranean Diet's focus on plant-based foods and fermented options nurtures a balanced gut microbiome, which is linked to reduced inflammation.

Anti-Inflammatory Nutrients: The diet's array of nutrients—such as curcumin in turmeric, quercetin in onions, and resveratrol in red wine—have been extensively studied for their potent anti-inflammatory effects.

Crafting a Balanced Plate: Nutrient-Rich Guidelines

This delves into the nuanced palette of choices that yield not only culinary delight but also nourishment that fuels vitality.

Begin by envisioning your plate as a canvas, divided into vibrant segments. Fill half with an array of colorful vegetables and fruits, a treasure trove of vitamins, minerals, and antioxidants. Embellish another quarter with lean proteins like fish, poultry, or legumes, infusing your plate with amino acids and healthy fats.

Complete your masterpiece with whole grains, occupying the final quarter, offering complex carbohydrates for sustained energy and fiber for gut health. A drizzle of extra virgin olive oil, a sprinkle of herbs and spices, and a handful of nuts or seeds add the final touches—a tapestry of flavors, colors, and nutrients that beckon to both your senses and your well-being.

Chapter 2

The Building Blocks of Flavorful Wellness

Superstar Ingredients of the Mediterranean Pantry

Olive Oil: Liquid Gold for Health

The elixir of Mediterranean cuisine, rich in monounsaturated fats and antioxidants, this golden oil is the cornerstone of heart health and inflammation reduction.

Yummy Fruits and Veggies: A Rainbow of Nutrients

From deep greens to vibrant reds, the Mediterranean pantry brims with fresh produce, offering an array of vitamins, minerals, and fiber that nourish the body and ward off diseases.

Whole Grains: Nourishing Your Body from Within

Nutrient-dense options like whole wheat, barley, and bulgur grace the Mediterranean table, supplying energy, fiber, and essential nutrients for sustained well-being.

Lean Proteins and Plant-Powered Alternatives

Fish and seafood, abundant in omega-3 fatty acids, form the heart of Mediterranean protein sources. Legumes and beans offer plant-based protein alternatives, fostering heart health and balanced nutrition.

Poultry and Lean Meats: Balancing Protein Intake

Poultry, such as chicken and turkey, takes center stage as lean, low-fat sources of protein. Their adaptability in various dishes, from succulent grilled kebabs to nourishing soups, showcases their culinary prowess. These meats provide essential amino acids that aid in muscle repair, growth, and overall bodily functions.

Lean meats, like lean cuts of beef or pork, can also be embraced in moderation. Opt for grass-fed and pasture-raised options whenever possible to maximize nutrient content. These meats offer essential nutrients, including iron and vitamin B12, while keeping saturated fat levels in check.

Unveiling the Magic of Herbs and Spices: Anti-Inflammatory Elixirs

Each pinch and sprinkle add not just taste, but a touch of health-promoting and culinary alchemy.

Basil: The fragrant basil leaf adds a burst of freshness to pasta, salads, and sauces, while its antioxidants contribute to an anti-inflammatory boost.

Oregano: With its robust aroma, oregano is more than a pizza topping. Rich in antioxidants, it offers potential health benefits, from immune support to combating oxidative stress.

Thyme: This delicate herb boasts a woodsy aroma and anti-inflammatory compounds. It adds depth to roasted dishes, stews, and marinades.

Rosemary: A fragrant companion to roasted meats and vegetables, rosemary's antioxidants and anti-inflammatory properties make it a staple in the Mediterranean kitchen.

Turmeric: The golden-hued spice, revered for curcumin's anti-inflammatory prowess, brightens dishes while offering potential health benefits.

Garlic: This pungent bulb is celebrated not only for its flavor but also for its immune-boosting and heart-protective qualities.

Cinnamon: Beyond its sweet allure, cinnamon offers potential benefits for blood sugar regulation and heart health.

Ginger: Its zingy heat is coupled with anti-inflammatory compounds that contribute to digestive comfort and overall well-being.

Chapter 3
From Breakfast to Brunch: Energizing Mornings

Sunrise Smoothie Bowl with Berries and Almonds

Serves: 1/Prep Time: 5 minutes

Ingredients:

- 1 frozen banana
- 1/2 cup mixed berries (blueberries, strawberries, raspberries)
- 1/2 cup unsweetened almond milk
- 1 tablespoon almond butter
- Toppings: sliced almonds, chia seeds, fresh berries

Instructions

1. In a blender, combine frozen bananas, mixed berries, almond milk, and almond butter.
2. Adding additional almond milk as necessary, blend until emulsified and creamy.
3. Pour the smoothie into a bowl.
4. Top with sliced almonds, chia seeds, and fresh berries.

Nutrition (per serving):

Calories: 300/Protein: 7g/Carbohydrates: 45g/Fat: 12g/Fiber: 10g

Mediterranean Veggie Omelet with Fresh Herbs

Serves: 1/Prep Time: 10 minutes/Cooking Time: 10 minutes

Ingredients:

- 2 large eggs
- 1/4 cup diced tomatoes
- 1/4 cup chopped spinach
- 2 tablespoons diced red onion
- 1 tablespoon chopped fresh basil
- Salt and pepper to taste
- 1 tablespoon crumbled feta cheese
- 1 teaspoon extra virgin olive oil

Instructions:

1. In a bowl, whisk the eggs until well beaten. Season with salt and pepper.
2. In a non-stick skillet, heat olive oil over medium heat.
3. Add diced onion and sauté until softened.
4. Add tomatoes and spinach; cook for 1-2 minutes until wilted.
5. Pour the beaten eggs evenly over the veggies. Let it cook for a minute.
6. Sprinkle fresh basil and feta cheese on one half of the omelet.
7. Gently fold the other half of the omelet over the filling.
8. To properly cook the eggs, heat for an additional 2-3 minutes.
9. Serve the omelet by sliding it onto a plate.

Nutrition (per serving):

Calories: 250/Protein: 18g/Carbohydrates: 10g/Fat: 16g/Fiber: 2g

Wholesome Quinoa Porridge with Dates and Nuts

Serves: 2/Prep Time: 5 minutes/Cooking Time: 15 minutes

Ingredients:

- 1/2 cup quinoa (rinsed)
- 1 cup water
- 1 cup unsweetened almond milk
- 1/4 teaspoon cinnamon
- 1/4 teaspoon vanilla extract
- 1/4 cup chopped nuts (walnuts, almonds)

- 1/4 cup chopped dates

- 1 tablespoon honey or maple syrup

Instructions:

In a saucepan, combine quinoa, water, almond milk, cinnamon, and vanilla extract.

Bring to a boil, then lower the heat and simmer the quinoa for fifteen minutes, or until it is tender.

Fluff the quinoa with a fork and divide it into bowls.

Top with chopped nuts, dates, and a drizzle of honey or maple syrup.

Nutrition (per serving):

Calories: 300/Protein: 8g/Carbohydrates: 45g/Fat: 10g/Fiber: 5g

Mediterranean Avocado Toast with Poached Egg

Serves: 1/Prep Time: 10 minutes/Cooking Time: 5 minutes

Ingredients:

- 1 slice gluten-free whole grain bread
- 1 ripe avocado, mashed
- 1 poached egg
- 1 tablespoon chopped fresh parsley
- 1 teaspoon lemon juice
- Salt and pepper to taste

- Red pepper flakes (optional)

Instructions:

Toast the gluten-free bread.

Spread the mashed avocado over the toasted bread.

Poach the egg: Bring a pot of water to a gentle simmer. Add a splash of vinegar. In a small bowl, crack one egg, and then carefully lower it into the heating water. A runny yolk requires roughly 3–4 minutes of cooking.

Use a slotted spoon to carefully remove the poached egg from the water and place it on top of the avocado.

Drizzle with lemon juice, and sprinkle chopped parsley, salt, and pepper.

If desired, add a small amount of red pepper flakes.

Nutrition (per serving):

Calories: 270/Protein: 10g/Carbohydrates: 18g/Fat: 18g/Fiber: 8g

Greek Yogurt and Fruit Parfait with Nutty Granola

Serves: 1/Prep Time: 10 minutes

Ingredients:

- 1/2 cup Greek yogurt (unsweetened)
- 1/2 cup mixed fresh fruits (kiwi, pineapple, mango)
- 1/4 cup gluten-free granola (with nuts and seeds)
- 1 tablespoon chopped mixed nuts (walnuts, pistachios)

- 1 teaspoon honey (optional)

Instructions:

In a glass or bowl, layer half of the Greek yogurt.

Add half of the mixed fresh fruits.

Sprinkle a layer of granola and chopped nuts.

Repeat the layers with the remaining ingredients.

If desired, add a drizzle of honey to the finish.

Nutrition (per serving):

Calories: 350/Protein: 15g/Carbohydrates: 45g/Fat: 12g/Fiber: 6g

Mediterranean Shakshuka with Spinach and Feta

Serves: 2/Prep Time: 10 minutes/Cooking Time: 20 minutes

Ingredients:

- 4 large eggs

- 1 tablespoon extra-virgin olive oil

- 1 onion, chopped

- 2 cloves garlic, minced

- 1 teaspoon ground cumin

- 1 teaspoon paprika

- 1/2 teaspoon ground coriander

- 1/4 teaspoon red pepper flakes (adjust to taste)

- 1 cup diced tomatoes (canned or fresh)

- 2 cups fresh spinach

- 1/4 cup crumbled feta cheese

- Salt and pepper to taste

- Chopped fresh parsley for garnish

Instructions:

1. Heat olive oil in a skillet, over medium heat. Add chopped onion and sauté until translucent.

2. Add minced garlic, ground cumin, paprika, ground coriander, and red pepper flakes. Cook for a minute until fragrant.

3. Add diced tomatoes and cook for about 5 minutes until they start to soften and form a sauce.

4. Create small wells in the tomato mixture and crack an egg into each well.

5. Scatter fresh spinach around the eggs. Cover the skillet and cook for about 5-7 minutes until the egg whites are set.

6. Sprinkle crumbled feta cheese over the shakshuka.

7. Season with salt and pepper, and garnish with chopped fresh parsley.

8. Serve the shakshuka warm.

Nutrition (per serving):

Calories: 230/Protein: 12g/Carbohydrates: 12g/Fat: 15g/Fiber: 4g

Coconut Chia Pudding with Mango and Pistachios

Serves: 2/Prep Time: 10 minutes (plus chilling time)/Cooking Time: 0 minutes

Ingredients:

- 1/4 cup chia seeds

- 1 cup of coconut milk (canned or carton)

- 2 tablespoons honey or maple syrup

- 1/2 teaspoon vanilla extract

- 1 ripe mango, diced

- 2 tablespoons chopped pistachios

Instructions:

1. Whisk together chia seeds, coconut milk, honey or maple syrup, and vanilla extract in a bowl.

2. Cover the bowl and refrigerate for at least 4 hours or overnight, until the mixture thickens.

3. When ready to serve, layer the chia pudding and diced mango in serving glasses.

4. Sprinkle chopped pistachios over the top.

Nutrition (per serving):

Calories: 300/Protein: 6g/Carbohydrates: 30g/Fat: 19g/Fiber: 10g

Quinoa Breakfast Bowl with Roasted Vegetables and Hummus

Serves: 2/Prep Time: 15 minutes/Cooking Time: 30 minutes

Ingredients:

- 1 cup cooked quinoa

- 1 cup mixed roasted vegetables (bell peppers, zucchini, cherry tomatoes)

- 1/2 cup hummus

- 2 large eggs, poached or fried

- Fresh parsley for garnish

- Lemon wedges for serving

Instructions:

1. Follow the directions on the quinoa package to prepare it.

2. Toss the roasted vegetables with a drizzle of olive oil, salt, and pepper. Roast in the oven until tender.

3. Assemble the bowls by dividing the cooked quinoa between two serving plates.

4. Top with roasted vegetables, a dollop of hummus, and a poached or fried egg.

5. Add fresh parsley as a garnish and serve with lemon wedges.

Nutrition (per serving):

Calories: 350/Protein: 16g/Carbohydrates: 36g/Fat: 15g/Fiber: 9g

Greek Yogurt and Almond Butter Stuffed Dates

Serves: 2/Prep Time: 10 minutes/Cooking Time: 0 minutes

Ingredients:

- 8 Medjool dates, pitted

- 1/4 cup Greek yogurt

- 2 tablespoons almond butter

- 1 tablespoon honey

- Chopped almonds for garnish

Instructions:

1. In a small bowl, mix Greek yogurt and almond butter until well combined.

2. Open each date and stuff it with a spoonful of the yogurt-almond butter mixture.

3. Drizzle honey over the stuffed dates.

4. Garnish with chopped almonds.

Nutrition (per serving):

Calories: 220/Protein: 4g/Carbohydrates: 46g/Fat: 6g/Fiber: 5g

Brunching the Mediterranean Way

Smashed Avocado Toast on Gluten-Free Whole Grain Bread

Serves: 1/Prep Time: 5 minutes

Ingredients:

- 2 slices gluten-free whole grain bread, toasted
- 1 ripe avocado

- 1 teaspoon lemon juice
- Salt and pepper to taste
- Red pepper flakes (optional)
- Fresh herbs (such as cilantro or parsley)

Instructions:

1. In a bowl, smash the avocado with lemon juice, salt, and pepper.
2. Spread the smashed avocado over the toasted bread slices.
3. Sprinkle red pepper flakes for a touch of heat.
4. Garnish with fresh herbs.

Nutrition (per serving):

Calories: 300/Protein: 5g/Carbohydrates: 25g/Fat: 20g/Fiber: 10g

Spinach and Feta Frittata Bursting with Flavor

Serves: 4/Prep Time: 10 minutes/Cooking Time: 20 minutes

Ingredients:

- 8 large eggs
- 1 cup fresh spinach, chopped
- 1/2 cup crumbled feta cheese
- 1/4 cup diced red onion
- 1/4 cup diced red bell pepper
- 1 teaspoon olive oil

- Salt and pepper to taste

Instructions:

1. Preheat the oven to 375°F (190°C).

2. In an oven-safe skillet, heat olive oil over medium heat.

3. Add the diced red bell pepper and onion and cook until softened.

4. Add chopped spinach; cook for 2-3 minutes until wilted.

5. In a bowl, whisk eggs, feta cheese, salt, and pepper.

6. Over the veggies in the skillet, pour the egg mixture.

7. Cook on the stovetop for 2-3 minutes until the edges start to set.

8. Transfer the skillet to the preheated oven and bake for 12-15 minutes until the frittata is fully set.

9. Remove from the oven, let it cool slightly, then slice and serve.

Nutrition (per serving):

Calories: 180/Protein: 12g/Carbohydrates: 4g/Fat: 13g/Fiber: 1g

Mediterranean Chickpea Flour Pancakes with Roasted Red Pepper Sauce

Serves: 2/Prep Time: 15 minutes/Cooking Time: 15 minutes

Ingredients for Pancakes:

- 1 cup chickpea flour
- 1/2 teaspoon ground cumin
- 1/2 teaspoon ground turmeric
- 1/4 teaspoon baking soda
- 1/4 teaspoon salt
- 3/4 cup water

- 2 tablespoons chopped fresh parsley
- 1/4 cup diced red onion

Ingredients for Roasted Red Pepper Sauce:

- 1 roasted red pepper (from a jar or freshly roasted)
- 1/4 cup Greek yogurt
- 1 clove garlic
- 1 tablespoon lemon juice
- Salt and pepper to taste

Instructions:

1. In a bowl, whisk the chickpea flour, cumin, turmeric, baking soda, and salt.
2. Gradually add water to form a smooth batter. Stir in chopped parsley and diced red onion.
3. Heat a non-stick skillet over medium heat. Pour a ladle of batter to make a pancake.
4. Cook until surface bubbles appear, then turn and continue to cook the other side until golden.
5. For the sauce, blend roasted red pepper, Greek yogurt, garlic, lemon juice, salt, and pepper until smooth.

6. Serve the chickpea flour pancakes with the roasted red pepper sauce.

Nutrition (per serving):

Calories: 280/Protein: 15g/Carbohydrates: 32g/Fat: 10g/Fiber: 8g

Smashed Avocado and Roasted Red Pepper Tartine

Serves: 2/Prep Time: 10 minutes/Cooking Time: 15 minutes

Ingredients:

- 2 slices gluten-free toasted, whole grain bread

- 1 ripe avocado, smashed

- 1 roasted red pepper, sliced

- 2 tablespoons crumbled feta cheese

- Fresh basil leaves for garnish

- Salt and pepper to taste

Instructions:

1. Spread the smashed avocado evenly over the toasted bread slices.

2. Top with sliced roasted red pepper.

3. Sprinkle crumbled feta cheese over the toppings.

4. Garnish with fresh basil leaves.

5. Add salt and pepper to taste.

Nutrition (per serving):

Calories: 280/Protein: 7g/Carbohydrates: 26g/Fat: 18g/Fiber: 7g

Quinoa and Veggie Stuffed Bell Peppers

Serves: 4/Prep Time: 20 minutes/Cooking Time: 30 minutes

Ingredients:

- 2 large bell peppers, halved and seeds removed

- 1 cup cooked quinoa

- 1 cup mixed roasted vegetables (zucchini, eggplant, red onion)

- 1/2 cup crumbled goat cheese

- 2 tablespoons chopped fresh parsley

- 1 tablespoon extra-virgin olive oil

- Salt and pepper to taste

Instructions:

1. Preheat the oven to 375°F (190°C).

2. Place the bell pepper halves on a baking sheet.

3. In a bowl, mix cooked quinoa, roasted vegetables, crumbled goat cheese, chopped parsley, olive oil, salt, and pepper.

4. Stuff the quinoa and vegetable mixture into the bell pepper halves.

5. Bake for about 25-30 minutes until the peppers are tender.

6. Serve the stuffed bell peppers warm.

Nutrition (per serving):

Calories: 250/Protein: 10g/Carbohydrates: 25g/Fat: 12g/Fiber: 5g

Mediterranean Frittata with Sun-Dried Tomatoes and Kalamata Olives

Serves: 4/Prep Time: 15 minutes/Cooking Time: 20 minutes

Ingredients:

- 8 large eggs

- 1/4 cup almond milk (or any non-dairy milk)

- 1/4 cup chopped sun-dried tomatoes

- 1/4 cup chopped Kalamata olives

- 1/4 cup crumbled feta cheese

- 2 tablespoons chopped fresh parsley

- 1 tablespoon extra-virgin olive oil

- Salt and pepper to taste

Instructions:

1. Preheat the oven to 375°F (190°C).

2. In a bowl, whisk together eggs and almond milk. Season with salt and pepper.

3. Heat olive oil in an oven-safe skillet over medium heat.

4. Add sun-dried tomatoes and Kalamata olives to the skillet and sauté for a minute.

5. Pour the egg mixture into the skillet and let it cook for a few minutes until the edges start to set.

6. Sprinkle crumbled feta cheese over the frittata.

7. Transfer the skillet to the preheated oven and bake for about 15 minutes or until the frittata is set and slightly golden.

8. Garnish with chopped fresh parsley.

9. Slice and serve the frittata warm.

Nutrition (per serving):

Calories: 210/Protein: 13g/Carbohydrates: 6g/Fat: 15gFiber: 2g

Chickpea Flour Pancakes with Tomato and Olive Salsa

Serves: 2/Prep Time: 15 minutes/Cooking Time: 15 minutes

Ingredients for Pancakes:

- 1 cup chickpea flour

- 1 teaspoon ground cumin

- 1/2 teaspoon ground turmeric

- 1/4 teaspoon baking soda

- 1/4 teaspoon salt

- 1 cup water

Ingredients for Tomato and Olive Salsa:

- 1 cup diced tomatoes

- 1/4 cup chopped Kalamata olives

- 2 tablespoons chopped fresh parsley

- 1 tablespoon extra-virgin olive oil

- 1 teaspoon lemon juice

- Salt and pepper to taste

Instructions:

1. In a bowl, whisk together the chickpea flour, ground cumin, ground turmeric, baking soda, salt, and water to form a smooth batter.

2. Heat a non-stick skillet over medium heat. To make a pancake, pour a ladleful of batter onto the skillet.

3. Cook for a few minutes on each side until the pancakes are golden and cooked through.

4. In a separate bowl, mix diced tomatoes, chopped Kalamata olives, chopped parsley, olive oil, lemon juice, salt, and pepper to make the salsa.

5. Serve the chickpea flour pancakes topped with the tomato and olive salsa.

Nutrition (per serving):

Calories: 300/Protein: 14g/Carbohydrates: 35g/Fat: 13g/Fiber: 8g

Chapter 4

Lively Lunches: Vibrant Midday Delights

Hearty Greek Salad with Grilled Chicken and Feta

Serves: 2/Prep Time: 15 minutes/Cooking Time: 15 minutes.

Ingredients:

- 2 boneless, skinless chicken breasts

- 1 teaspoon dried oregano
- Salt and pepper to taste
- 4 cups mixed salad greens
- 1 cup cherry tomatoes, halved
- 1 cucumber, sliced
- 1/2 red onion, thinly sliced
- 1/4 cup kalamata olives
- 1/4 cup crumbled feta cheese
- 2 tablespoons extra virgin olive oil
- 2 tablespoons balsamic vinegar

Instructions:

1. Season chicken breasts with dried oregano, salt, and pepper.
2. Grill the chicken on medium heat for about 6-7 minutes per side or until cooked through.
3. In a large bowl, combine salad greens, cherry tomatoes, cucumber, red onion, and kalamata olives.
4. Slice the grilled chicken and place it on top of the salad.
5. Sprinkle crumbled feta cheese over the salad.
6. Whisk together olive oil and balsamic vinegar to make the dressing.
7. Drizzle the dressing over the salad before serving.

Nutrition (per serving):

Calories: 400/Protein: 30g/Carbohydrates: 15g/Fat: 25g/Fiber: 4g

Quinoa and Roasted Veggie Salad with Balsamic Vinaigrette

Serves: 4/Prep Time: 15 minutes/Cooking Time: 25 minutes

Ingredients:

- 1 cup quinoa
- 2 cups mixed roasted vegetables (bell peppers, zucchini, eggplant)

- 1/4 cup chopped fresh parsley
- 1/4 cup crumbled goat cheese
- 2 tablespoons balsamic vinegar
- 2 tablespoons extra virgin olive oil
- Salt and pepper to taste

Instructions:

1. Cook the quinoa according to package instructions and allow it cool.
2. Preheat the oven to 400°F (200°C). Toss mixed vegetables with olive oil, salt, and pepper. Roast for about 20-25 minutes until tender.
3. In a large bowl, combine cooked quinoa, roasted vegetables, chopped parsley, and crumbled goat cheese.
4. Whisk balsamic vinegar, olive oil, salt, and pepper all together to make the dressing.
5. Drizzle the dressing over the quinoa and roasted veggie mixture. Toss to combine.

Nutrition (per serving):

Calories: 320/Protein: 9g/Carbohydrates: 40g/Fat: 15g/Fiber: 7g

White Bean and Tuna Salad with Lemon-Herb Dressing

Serves: 2/Prep Time: 10 minutes

Ingredients:

- 1 can (15 oz) drained and rinsed white beans
- 1 can (5 oz) tuna, drained
- 1/4 cup chopped red onion
- 1/4 cup chopped fresh parsley
- 1/4 cup chopped fresh dill

- Zest and juice of 1 lemon
- 2 tablespoons extra virgin olive oil
- Salt and pepper to taste

Instructions:

1. In a bowl, combine white beans, tuna, red onion, parsley, and dill.
2. In a separate bowl, whisk together lemon zest, lemon juice, olive oil, salt, and pepper.
3. Pour the dressing over the bean and tuna mixture. Toss to combine.

Nutrition (per serving):

Calories: 350/Protein: 25g/Carbohydrates: 30g/Fat: 15g/Fiber: 10g

Falafel and Hummus Bowl with Cucumber-Tomato Relish

Serves: 2/Prep Time: 20 minutes/Cooking Time: 15 minutes

Ingredients:

- 8 falafel patties (store-bought or homemade)
- 1 cup hummus
- 1 cup cooked quinoa
- 1 cup diced cucumber
- 1 cup diced cherry tomatoes
- 1/4 cup chopped fresh mint

- 1/4 cup chopped fresh parsley
- Juice of 1 lemon
- Salt and pepper to taste

Instructions:

1. Heat falafel patties according to package instructions or cook homemade falafel.
2. In a bowl, combine diced cucumber, diced cherry tomatoes, chopped mint, chopped parsley, lemon juice, salt, and pepper to make the relish.
3. In serving bowls, assemble the bowls by layering hummus, cooked quinoa, falafel patties, and the cucumber-tomato relish.

Nutrition (per serving):

Calories: 480/Protein: 15g/Carbohydrates: 55g/Fat: 25g/Fiber: 12g

Grilled Eggplant and Quinoa Bowl with Tahini Drizzle

Serves: 2/Prep Time: 15 minutes/Cooking Time: 15 minutes

Ingredients:

- 1 medium eggplant, sliced
- 1 cup cooked quinoa
- 1/4 cup chopped fresh mint
- 1/4 cup chopped fresh parsley
- 1/4 cup crumbled feta cheese

- 2 tablespoons tahini
- 2 tablespoons lemon juice
- 1 tablespoon extra-virgin olive oil
- Salt and pepper to taste

Instructions:

1. Preheat a grill or grill pan. Brush eggplant slices with olive oil and season with salt and pepper. Grill for about 2-3 minutes per side until tender and charred.
2. In a bowl, whisk together tahini, lemon juice, olive oil, salt, and pepper to make the dressing.
3. In serving bowls, assemble the bowls by layering cooked quinoa, grilled eggplant slices, chopped mint, chopped parsley, and crumbled feta cheese. Drizzle with tahini dressing.

Nutrition (per serving):

Calories: 350/Protein: 12g/Carbohydrates: 40g/Fat: 18g/Fiber: 10g

Lentil and Brown Rice Bowl with Yogurt-Mint Sauce

Serves: 2/Prep Time: 15 minutes/Cooking Time: 25 minutes

Ingredients:

- 1 cup cooked brown rice
- 1 cup cooked green or brown lentils
- 1 cup diced cucumber
- 1/2 cup diced red bell pepper
- 1/4 cup chopped fresh mint

- 1/4 cup chopped fresh parsley
- 1/2 cup plain Greek yogurt
- 1 tablespoon lemon juice
- 1 tablespoon extra-virgin olive oil
- Salt and pepper to taste

Instructions:

1. In a bowl, combine cooked brown rice, cooked lentils, diced cucumber, diced red bell pepper, chopped mint, and chopped parsley.
2. In a separate bowl, whisk together Greek yogurt, lemon juice, olive oil, salt, and pepper to make the sauce.
3. Serve the lentil and rice mixture in bowls, and drizzle with yogurt-mint sauce.

Nutrition (per serving):

Calories: 380/Protein: 18g/Carbohydrates: 60g/Fat: 8g/Fiber: 12g

Chapter 5
Captivating Dinners: Savoring Evening Comfort

Seafood Sensations

Baked Salmon with Dill and Lemon Zest

Serves: 2/Prep Time: 10 minutes/Cooking Time: 20 minutes

Ingredients:

- 2 salmon fillets
- 2 tablespoons fresh dill, chopped
- Zest of 1 lemon
- 2 tablespoons extra virgin olive oil
- Salt and pepper to taste

Instructions:

1. Preheat the oven to 375°F (190°C).
2. On a baking sheet covered with parchment paper, put the salmon fillets.
3. In a bowl, mix chopped dill, lemon zest, olive oil, salt, and pepper.
4. Spread the dill mixture evenly over the salmon fillets.
5. Bake in the preheated oven for 15 to 20 minutes, or until the salmon flakes with a fork without difficulty.
6. Serve the baked salmon with a side dish of your choice

Nutrition (per serving):

Calories: 350/Protein: 30g/Carbohydrates: 0g/Fat: 24g/Fiber: 0g

Garlic and Herb Grilled Shrimp with Mediterranean Quinoa

Serves: 2/Prep Time: 15 minutes/Cooking Time: 20 minutes

Ingredients for Shrimp:

- 1/2-pound large shrimp, peeled and deveined
- 2 cloves garlic, minced
- 1 tablespoon chopped fresh parsley
- 1 tablespoon chopped fresh oregano
- 2 tablespoons extra virgin olive oil

- Juice of 1 lemon
- Salt and pepper to taste

Ingredients for Quinoa:

- 1 cup cooked quinoa
- 1/4 cup diced cucumber
- 1/4 cup diced red bell pepper
- 1/4 cup chopped kalamata olives
- 2 tablespoons crumbled feta cheese
- 2 tablespoons chopped fresh parsley

Instructions:

1. Preheat the grill to medium-high heat.
2. In a bowl, mix garlic, parsley, oregano, olive oil, lemon juice, salt, and pepper.
3. Thread the shrimp onto skewers and brush them with the garlic and herb mixture.
4. Grill the shrimp for two to three minutes on each side, or until fully done.
5. In a separate bowl, combine cooked quinoa, diced cucumber, diced red bell pepper, kalamata olives, crumbled feta cheese, and chopped parsley.

6. Serve the grilled shrimp over the Mediterranean quinoa.

Nutrition (per serving):

Calories: 400/Protein: 25g/Carbohydrates: 30g/Fat: 20g/Fiber: 6g

Seared Cod with Olive Tapenade and Roasted Vegetables

Serves: 2/Prep Time: 15 minutes/Cooking Time: 20 minutes

Ingredients for Cod:

- 2 cod fillets
- 2 tablespoons olive tapenade
- 1 tablespoon extra-virgin olive oil
- Juice of 1 lemon
- Salt and pepper to taste

Ingredients for Roasted Vegetables:

- 2 cups of mixed vegetables (zucchini, bell peppers, cherry tomatoes)
- 2 tablespoons extra virgin olive oil
- 1 teaspoon dried oregano
- Salt and pepper to taste

Instructions:

1. Preheat the oven to 400°F (200°C).
2. On a baking sheet covered with parchment paper, put the cod fillets.
3. Spread olive tapenade over the cod fillets.
4. Drizzle with olive oil and lemon juice. Season with salt and pepper.
5. Toss mixed vegetables with olive oil, dried oregano, salt, and pepper. Spread on a separate baking sheet.

6. Roast the cod and vegetables in the preheated oven for about 15-20 minutes until the fish flakes easily and the vegetables are tender.

7. Serve the seared cod with olive tapenade alongside the roasted vegetables.

Nutrition (per serving):

Calories: 350/Protein: 30g/Carbohydrates: 15g/Fat: 18g/Fiber: 5g

Grilled Lemon-Herb Salmon with Quinoa and Roasted Vegetables

Serves: 2/Prep Time: 15 minutes/Cooking Time: 20 minutes

Ingredients:

- 2 salmon fillets

- Juice of 1 lemon

- 2 tablespoons extra virgin olive oil

- 2 cloves garlic, minced

- 1 teaspoon dried oregano

- 1 teaspoon dried thyme

- Salt and pepper to taste

- 1 cup cooked quinoa

- 2 cups mixed roasted vegetables (bell peppers, zucchini, cherry tomatoes)

- Chopped fresh parsley for garnish

Instructions:

1. In a bowl, mix lemon juice, olive oil, minced garlic, dried oregano, dried thyme, salt, and pepper.

2. Spread the marinade over the salmon fillets in a shallow dish. For about 15 minutes, let them marinade.

3. Preheat the grill to medium-high heat.

4. Grill the salmon fillets for about 4-5 minutes on each side, or until cooked to your desired level of doneness.

5. In a serving plate, arrange the cooked quinoa and roasted vegetables.

6. Place the grilled salmon fillets on top.

7. Garnish with chopped fresh parsley.

8. Serve the dish warm.

Nutrition (per serving):

Calories: 400/Protein: 30g/Carbohydrates: 35g/Fat: 16g/Fiber: 6g

Mediterranean Baked Cod with Olive and Tomato Relish

Serves: 2/Prep Time: 15 minutes/Cooking Time: 20 minutes

Ingredients:

- 2 cod fillets

- 1 tablespoon extra-virgin olive oil

- 1 teaspoon dried oregano

- 1 teaspoon dried basil

- Salt and pepper to taste

- 1 cup cherry tomatoes, halved

- 1/4 cup Kalamata olives, pitted and chopped

- 2 tablespoons chopped fresh parsley

- Juice of 1 lemon

Instructions:

1. Preheat the oven to 375°F (190°C).
2. Put the cod fillets in a baking dish.
3. Drizzle olive oil over the fillets and sprinkle with dried oregano, dried basil, salt, and pepper.
4. Bake in the preheated oven for about 15-20 minutes, or until the cod is cooked through and flakes easily.
5. In a bowl, mix cherry tomatoes, chopped Kalamata olives, chopped parsley, and lemon juice to make the relish.
6. Serve the baked cod fillets topped with the olive and tomato relish.

Nutrition (per serving):

Calories: 300/Protein: 30g/Carbohydrates: 10g/Fat: 15g/Fiber: 3g

Garlic-Lemon Herb Grilled Shrimp with Quinoa and Arugula Salad

Serves: 2/Prep Time: 15 minutes/Cooking Time: 10 minutes

Ingredients for Grilled Shrimp:

- 1/2-pound large shrimp (peeled and deveined)

- 2 cloves garlic, minced

- Juice of 1 lemon

- 2 tablespoons extra virgin olive oil

- 1 teaspoon dried thyme

- Salt and pepper to taste

Ingredients for Quinoa and Arugula Salad:

- 1 cup cooked quinoa
- 2 cups arugula
- 1/4 cup crumbled feta cheese
- 1/4 cup cherry tomatoes, halved
- 2 tablespoons chopped fresh basil
- Juice of 1 lemon
- 1 tablespoon extra-virgin olive oil

Instructions:

1. In a bowl, mix minced garlic, lemon juice, olive oil, dried thyme, salt, and pepper.
2. Toss the shrimp in the marinade and let them marinate for about 10 minutes.
3. Preheat the grill to medium-high heat.
4. Grill the shrimp for about 2-3 minutes on each side, until they are opaque and cooked through.
5. In a separate bowl, combine cooked quinoa, arugula, crumbled feta cheese, cherry tomatoes, chopped basil, lemon juice, and olive oil to make the salad.
6. Serve the grilled shrimp over the quinoa and arugula salad.

Nutrition (per serving):

Calories: 350/Protein: 30g/Carbohydrates: 25g/Fat: 15g/Fiber: 4g

Seared Scallops with Roasted Vegetable Medley

Serves: 2/Prep Time: 15 minutes/Cooking Time: 20 minutes

Ingredients:

- 10-12 large scallops, patted dry

- 2 tablespoons extra virgin olive oil

- 1 teaspoon dried rosemary

- 1/2 teaspoon paprika

- Salt and pepper to taste

- 2 cups mixed roasted vegetables (carrots, Brussels sprouts, red onion)

- Lemon wedges for serving

Instructions:

1. Preheat the oven to 400°F (200°C).

2. Toss the scallops with 1 tablespoon of olive oil, dried rosemary, paprika, salt, and pepper.

3. Heat the remaining 1 tablespoon of olive oil in a skillet over medium-high heat.

4. Sear the scallops for about 2-3 minutes on each side until they are golden and cooked through.

5. Meanwhile, roast the mixed vegetables in the preheated oven for about 15-20 minutes, until they are tender.

6. Serve the seared scallops over the roasted vegetable medley.

7. Squeeze lemon wedges over the dish before enjoying.

Nutrition (per serving):

Calories: 250/Protein: 20g/Carbohydrates: 15g/Fat: 12g/Fiber: 5g

Plant-Powered Dinners for Optimal Wellness

Mediterranean Stuffed Bell Peppers with Herbed Cauliflower Rice

Serves: 4/Prep Time: 20 minutes/Cooking Time: 35 minutes

Ingredients for Stuffed Peppers:

- 4 large bell peppers, (halved and seeds removed)
- 2 cups cauliflower rice (raw or pre-riced)
- 1 cup cooked chickpeas

- 1/2 cup chopped kalamata olives
- 1/2 cup crumbled feta cheese
- 1/4 cup chopped fresh parsley
- 1/4 cup chopped fresh mint
- 2 tablespoons extra virgin olive oil
- Salt and pepper to taste

Instructions:

1. Preheat the oven to 375°F (190°C).

2. In a bowl, mix cauliflower rice, cooked chickpeas, chopped olives, crumbled feta cheese, chopped parsley, chopped mint, olive oil, salt, and pepper.

3. Fill each bell pepper half with the cauliflower rice mixture.

4. Place stuffed peppers in a baking dish and cover with aluminum foil.

5. Bake in the preheated oven for about 25-30 minutes until the peppers are tender.

6. Take away the foil and bake for an additional 5 minutes to lightly brown the tops.

7. Serve the stuffed peppers warm.

Nutrition (per serving):

Calories: 230/Protein: 10g/Carbohydrates: 25g/Fat: 11g/Fiber: 7g

Zucchini Noodles with Cherry Tomato and Basil Sauce

Serves: 2/Prep Time: 15 minutes/Cooking Time: 15 minutes

Ingredients:

- 2 large zucchinis, spiralized into noodles
- 2 cups cherry tomatoes, halved

- 1/4 cup chopped fresh basil
- 2 cloves garlic, minced
- 2 tablespoons extra virgin olive oil
- Salt and pepper to taste
- Grated Parmesan cheese for garnish (optional)

Instructions:

1. In a skillet, heat olive oil over medium heat. Sauté the minced garlic for one minute, until fragrant.
2. Add halved cherry tomatoes to the skillet and cook for about 5-7 minutes until they start to soften and release their juices.
3. Stir in chopped basil, salt, and pepper.
4. Add zucchini noodles to the skillet and toss to combine. Allow to boil for 2-3 minutes until the noodles are heated through.
5. Divide the zucchini noodles and tomato sauce between serving plates.
6. Garnish with grated Parmesan cheese if desired.

Nutrition (per serving):

Calories: 180/Protein: 5g/Carbohydrates: 15g/Fat: 12g/Fiber: 4g

Lentil and Spinach Curry with Fragrant Turmeric Rice

Serves: 4/Prep Time: 15 minutes/Cooking Time: 35 minutes

Ingredients for Lentil Curry:

- 1 cup green or brown lentils, rinsed and drained
- 1 onion, finely chopped
- 2 cloves garlic, minced
- 1 teaspoon ground cumin
- 1 teaspoon ground coriander
- 1 teaspoon ground turmeric
- 1/2 teaspoon ground ginger

- 1/2 teaspoon ground cinnamon
- 1/4 teaspoon cayenne pepper (adjust to taste)
- 1 can (14 oz) diced tomatoes
- 1 can (14 oz) coconut milk
- 2 cups fresh spinach leaves
- 2 tablespoons olive oil
- Salt and pepper to taste

Ingredients for Fragrant Turmeric Rice:

- 1 cup basmati rice
- 2 cups water
- 1/2 teaspoon ground turmeric
- 1/4 teaspoon ground cumin
- Salt to taste

Instructions:

1. Heat olive oil over medium heat in a pot. Add chopped onion and sauté until translucent.
2. Add minced garlic, ground cumin, ground coriander, ground turmeric, ground ginger, ground cinnamon, and cayenne pepper. Cook for a minute until fragrant.

3. Add rinsed lentils, diced tomatoes, and coconut milk. Bring to a simmer and cook for about 20-25 minutes until the lentils are tender.
4. Stir in fresh spinach leaves and cook until wilted. Season with salt and pepper.
5. In a separate pot, cook basmati rice with water, ground turmeric, ground cumin, and salt according to package instructions.
6. Serve the lentil curry over fragrant turmeric rice.

Nutrition (per serving):

Calories: 450/Protein: 15g/Carbohydrates: 70g/Fat: 15g/Fiber: 14g

Lentil and Spinach Stuffed Bell Peppers

Serves: 4/Prep Time: 20 minutes/Cooking Time: 40 minutes

Ingredients:

- 4 large bell peppers (halved and seeds removed)

- 1 cup cooked green lentils

- 2 cups baby spinach, chopped

- 1 small onion, finely chopped

- 2 cloves garlic, minced

- 1 teaspoon ground cumin
- 1 teaspoon ground coriander
- 1/2 teaspoon smoked paprika
- Salt and pepper to taste
- 1/4 cup crumbled goat cheese (optional)
- Chopped fresh parsley for garnish

Instructions:

1. Preheat the oven to 375°F (190°C).
2. Place the bell pepper halves in a baking dish.
3. In a skillet, sauté chopped onion and minced garlic until translucent.
4. Add ground cumin, ground coriander, smoked paprika, salt, and pepper. Cook for a minute.
5. Stir in cooked lentils and chopped baby spinach. Allow to cook for a few minutes until the spinach wilts.
6. Stuff the bell pepper halves with the lentil and spinach mixture.
7. Sprinkle crumbled goat cheese over the top, if using.
8. Cover the baking dish with foil and bake for about 30 minutes.
9. Add chopped fresh parsley to garnish before serving.

Nutrition (per serving):

Calories: 220/Protein: 12g/Carbohydrates: 38g/Fat: 3g/Fiber: 14g

Mediterranean Chickpea and Vegetable Stir-Fry

Serves: 4/Prep Time: 15 minutes/Cooking Time: 20 minutes

Ingredients:

- 2 cups cooked chickpeas

- 2 cups mixed vegetables (bell peppers, zucchini, cherry tomatoes)

- 1 small red onion, thinly sliced

- 3 cloves garlic, minced

- 1 teaspoon dried oregano

- 1/2 teaspoon ground cumin

- Juice of 1 lemon

- 2 tablespoons extra virgin olive oil

- Salt and pepper to taste

- Chopped fresh parsley for garnish

Instructions:

1. Heat olive oil in a large skillet over medium heat.

2. Add sliced red onion and minced garlic. Sauté until the onion is translucent.

3. Add mixed vegetables to the skillet and cook for a few minutes until they start to soften.

4. Stir in cooked chickpeas, dried oregano, ground cumin, lemon juice, salt, and pepper.

5. Cook for another 5-7 minutes until the chickpeas are heated through and the flavors are well combined.

6. Add chopped fresh parsley to garnish before serving.

Nutrition (per serving):

Calories: 280/Protein: 11g/Carbohydrates: 40g/Fat: 9g/Fiber: 10g

Eggplant and Lentil Moussaka

Serves: 4/Prep Time: 30 minutes/Cooking Time: 45 minutes

Ingredients:

- 1 large eggplant, sliced into rounds
- 1 cup cooked green lentils
- 1 small onion, finely chopped
- 2 cloves garlic, minced
- 1 teaspoon ground cinnamon
- 1/2 teaspoon ground nutmeg
- 1/4 teaspoon ground cloves
- 2 cups tomato sauce
- 1/2 cup unsweetened almond milk
- 2 tablespoons nutritional yeast (optional)
- Salt and pepper to taste
- Chopped fresh parsley for garnish

Instructions:

1. Preheat the oven to 375°F (190°C).

2. Arrange eggplant slices on a baking sheet. Brush with olive oil and bake for about 15-20 minutes until they are tender.

3. In a skillet, sauté chopped onion and minced garlic until translucent.

4. Add ground cinnamon, ground nutmeg, ground cloves, salt, and pepper. Cook for a minute.

5. Stir in cooked lentils and tomato sauce. Simmer for about 10 minutes.

6. In a separate bowl, mix almond milk and nutritional yeast.

7. Layer half of the eggplant slices in a baking dish. Garnish with half of the lentil mixture.

8. Repeat the layers with the remaining eggplant and lentil mixture.

9. Pour the almond milk mixture over the top.

10. For about 25-30 minutes bake in the preheated oven until the moussaka is heated through and bubbly.

11. Garnish with chopped fresh parsley before serving.

Nutrition (per serving):

Calories: 280/Protein: 13g/Carbohydrates: 45g/Fat: 6g/Fiber: 12g

Mediterranean Roasted Cauliflower and Chickpea Bowl

Serves: 4/Prep Time: 15 minutes/Cooking Time: 30 minutes

Ingredients:

- 1 small head cauliflower (cut into florets)
- 2 cups cooked chickpeas
- 1 tablespoon ground cumin
- 1 teaspoon ground turmeric
- 1/2 teaspoon ground paprika
- 2 tablespoons extra virgin olive oil
- Salt and pepper to taste

- 4 cups mixed greens
- 1/4 cup crumbled feta cheese
- 2 tablespoons chopped fresh mint
- Juice of 1 lemon

Instructions:

1. Preheat the oven to 400°F (200°C).
2. In a bowl, toss cauliflower florets and cooked chickpeas with ground cumin, ground turmeric, ground paprika, olive oil, salt, and pepper.
3. Spread the mixture on a baking sheet and roast in the preheated oven for about 25-30 minutes until the cauliflower is golden and tender.
4. In a serving bowl, arrange mixed greens.
5. Top with the roasted cauliflower and chickpea mixture.
6. Sprinkle crumbled feta cheese and chopped fresh mint over the top.
7. Squeeze lemon juice over the bowl before serving.

Nutrition (per serving):

Calories: 320/Protein: 14g/Carbohydrates: 40g/Fat: 12g/Fiber: 12g

Chapter 6
Guilt-Free Mediterranean Desserts

Olive Oil and Orange Cake with Citrus Glaze

Serves: 8/Prep Time: 20 minutes/Cooking Time: 45 minutes

Ingredients for Cake:

- 1 1/2 cups all-purpose flour

- 1 cup granulated sugar
- 3 large eggs
- 1/2 cup extra virgin olive oil
- 1/2 cup fresh orange juice
- Zest of 1 orange
- 1 teaspoon baking powder
- 1/4 teaspoon salt

Ingredients for Citrus Glaze:

- 1 cup powdered sugar
- 2 tablespoons fresh orange juice
- Zest of 1 orange

Instructions:

1. Preheat the oven to 350°F (175°C). Grease and flour a cake pan.
2. Whisk together flour, baking powder, and salt in a bowl.
3. In another bowl, beat eggs and granulated sugar until pale and fluffy.
4. Gradually add olive oil, orange juice, and orange zest, mixing well.

5. Mix in the dry ingredients until just combined.

6. Fill the prepared cake pan with the batter, and bake for 40 to 45 minutes, or until a toothpick inserted in the center comes out clean.

7. The cake should cool in the pan for 10 minutes before being moved to a wire rack to finish cooling.

8. For the glaze, whisk together powdered sugar, orange juice, and orange zest until smooth.

9. Prior to serving, drizzle the glaze over the cake that has cooled.

Nutrition (per serving):

Calories: 320/Protein: 4g/Carbohydrates: 50g/Fat: 13g/Fiber: 1g

Almond Flour Chocolate Brownies with Sea Salt

Serves: 12/Prep Time: 15 minutes/Cooking Time: 25 minutes

Ingredients:

- 1 1/2 cups almond flour
- 1/3 cup cocoa powder
- 1/2 teaspoon baking soda
- 1/4 teaspoon salt

- 1/2 cup honey or maple syrup
- 1/4 cup extra virgin olive oil
- 2 large eggs
- 1 teaspoon vanilla extract
- 1/2 cup dark chocolate chips
- Sea salt flakes for topping

Instructions:

1. Preheat the oven to 350°F (175°C). Grease and line a baking pan with parchment paper.
2. In a bowl, whisk together almond flour, cocoa powder, baking soda, and salt.
3. In another bowl, whisk together honey or maple syrup, olive oil, eggs, and vanilla extract.
4. Combine the wet and dry ingredients, then fold in the dark chocolate chips.
5. Pour the batter into the prepared baking pan and smooth the top.
6. Bake for about 20-25 minutes until a toothpick inserted into the center comes out with a few moist crumbs.
7. While the brownies are still warm, top them with a sprinkle of sea salt.

8. Before slicing and serving the brownies, give them time to cool completely.

Nutrition (per serving):

Calories: 220/Protein: 4g/Carbohydrates: 20g/Fat: 15g/Fiber: 3g

Greek Yogurt Parfait with Honey and Fresh Berries

Serves: 2Prep Time: 10 minutes

Ingredients:

- 1 cup Greek yogurt
- 2 tablespoons honey
- 1 cup of mixed fresh berries (strawberries, blueberries, raspberries)
- 1/4 cup granola

Instructions:

1. In serving glasses or bowls, set in layers Greek yogurt, mixed berries, and granola.
2. Drizzle honey over the top of each parfait.
3. Repeat the layers and finish with a drizzle of honey.

Nutrition (per serving):

Calories: 200/Protein: 10g/Carbohydrates: 30g/Fat: 5g/Fiber: 4g

Chia Seed Pudding with Fresh Mango

Serves: 2/Prep Time: 10 minutes (plus chilling time) /Cooking Time: 0 minutes

Ingredients:

- 1/4 cup chia seeds
- 1 cup unsweetened almond milk
- 1 tablespoon honey or maple syrup
- 1/2 teaspoon vanilla extract
- 1 ripe mango, diced

Instructions:

1. In a bowl, whisk together chia seeds, almond milk, honey or maple syrup, and vanilla extract.

2. Cover the bowl and refrigerate for at least 4 hours or overnight, until the mixture thickens.

3. When ready to serve, layer the chia pudding and diced mango in serving glasses.

Nutrition (per serving):

Calories: 180/Protein: 4g/Carbohydrates: 25g/Fat: 7g/Fiber: 11g

Baked Apples with Cinnamon and Walnuts

Serves: 4/Prep Time: 10 minutes/Cooking Time: 30 minutes

Ingredients:

- 4 medium apples
- 1/4 cup chopped walnuts
- 2 tablespoons honey
- 1 teaspoon ground cinnamon
- 1/4 teaspoon ground nutmeg
- 1 tablespoon melted coconut oil

Instructions:

1. Preheat the oven to 350°F (175°C). Core the apples, leaving the bottoms intact.
2. In a bowl, mix chopped walnuts, honey, cinnamon, nutmeg, and melted coconut oil.
3. Place the apples in a baking dish after stuffing each one with the walnut mixture.
4. Bake the apples for about 25 to 30 minutes, or until they are soft.
5. Serve the baked apples warm.

Nutrition (per serving):

Calories: 180/Protein: 2g/Carbohydrates: 30g/Fat: 8g/Fiber: 5g

Greek Yogurt and Berry Frozen Pops

Makes: 6 popsicles/Prep Time: 10 minutes (plus freezing time)/Cooking Time: 0 minutes

Ingredients:

- 2 cups Greek yogurt
- 1 cup mixed berries (strawberries, blueberries, raspberries)
- 2 tablespoons honey
- 1 teaspoon vanilla extract

Instructions:

1. Combine Greek yogurt, mixed berries, honey, and vanilla extract in a blender. Blend until smooth.
2. Pour the mixture into popsicle molds.
3. Insert popsicle sticks and freeze for at least 4 hours or until fully frozen.
4. To remove the popsicles, briefly run the molds under warm water.

Nutrition (per serving - 1 popsicle):

Calories: 80/Protein: 6g/Carbohydrates: 12g/Fat: 1g/Fiber: 1g

Date and Nut Energy Bites

Makes: About 12 bites/Prep Time: 15 minutes/Cooking Time: 0 minutes

Ingredients:

- 1 cup pitted dates
- 1/2 cup nuts (such as almonds, walnuts, or cashews)
- 1/4 cup unsweetened shredded coconut
- 2 tablespoons cocoa powder
- 1 tablespoon honey or maple syrup

- 1 teaspoon vanilla extract
- Pinch of salt

Instructions:

1. In a food processor, combine pitted dates, nuts, shredded coconut, cocoa powder, honey or maple syrup, vanilla extract, and a pinch of salt.
2. Mixture should be processed until it resembles sticky dough.
3. Roll the dough into bite-sized balls.
4. The energy bites should be kept in the refrigerator in an airtight container.

Nutrition (per serving - 1 energy bite):

Calories: 80/Protein: 2g/Carbohydrates: 12g/Fat: 4g/Fiber: 2g

Conclusion

In concluding this journey through **The Anti-Inflammatory Mediterranean Diet Cookbook: 1500 Days of Nourishing and Tasty Gluten-Free Recipes to Help Reduce Inflammation and Boost Wellness,** we have explored the rich tapestry of flavors, nutrients, and health benefits that the Mediterranean diet offers. Through these pages, we embarked on a culinary expedition, uncovering the art of crafting meals that are both indulgent to the senses and nurturing to the body.

In the modern world, where our diets and lifestyles can often contribute to inflammation and compromised well-being, the Mediterranean diet stands as a beacon of wisdom. Its principles, rooted in the bountiful offerings of the Mediterranean region, teach us to embrace whole foods, vibrant produce, and healthful fats. The recipes presented in this cookbook harmoniously merge tradition with innovation, promising not only exquisite tastes but also a means to support our body's innate healing processes.

By delving into the mechanisms of inflammation, we recognized the critical role diet plays in fostering a balanced and resilient state of health. We unraveled the distinction between chronic and acute inflammation, enlightening ourselves on the effects that various foods can have on our bodies. While some foods act as silent culprits, fueling the flames of inflammation, others emerge as valiant heroes, fighting against it.

The Mediterranean diet's core principles emerged as a guiding light throughout these culinary explorations. The harmonious marriage of colorful vegetables, wholesome grains, lean proteins, and heart-healthy fats redefined our approach to nourishment. The intricate dance of flavors and textures that this diet offers demonstrates that wellness and indulgence need not be mutually exclusive.

The science behind the Mediterranean diet's anti-inflammatory benefits unveiled the profound impact this lifestyle can have on our overall well-being. From reducing the risk of chronic diseases to supporting cognitive health, the Mediterranean diet's influence extends beyond the plate, touching every facet of our lives.

Crafting a balanced plate emerged as an essential theme in this culinary odyssey. By adhering to nutrient-rich guidelines, we learned to approach meal preparation with mindfulness and intention. The ingredients we select and the combinations we create have the power to influence our health journey positively.

As we journeyed through these pages, we also explored the Mediterranean pantry's superstar ingredients, discovering the secret weapons that add depth, flavor, and nutritional prowess to our dishes. From olive oil's liquid gold to the magic of herbs and spices, we witnessed the transformation that these ingredients can bring to our culinary creations.

From hearty breakfasts to vibrant lunches and sumptuous dinners, this cookbook furnished a treasure trove of recipes that celebrate the Mediterranean diet's essence. Each dish is a symphony of nutrients, flavors, and aromas, reflecting the belief that food is a source of vitality and joy.

In the realm of desserts, we found a sweet sanctuary that aligns with the Mediterranean diet's principles. These guilt-free indulgences, rich in wholesome ingredients, tantalized our taste buds without compromising our health goals.

As the final pages of this cookbook are turned, let us carry the lessons learned here into our daily lives. Let the kitchen be our canvas, and the ingredients our palette. Let us savor the journey of crafting each meal, knowing that we are nurturing not only our bodies but our spirits as well. With each bite, we embrace a legacy of tradition and a commitment to wellness.

May The Anti-Inflammatory Mediterranean Diet Cookbook inspire us to embrace the Mediterranean way of life, fostering not only a healthier body but a profound appreciation for the beauty of wholesome, delicious, and nurturing cuisine. As we step away from these pages and into our kitchens, may we continue to honor the wisdom of the Mediterranean diet, celebrating the union of nourishment and pleasure that it offers.

Bonus Section
A Comprehensive List of Anti-Inflammatory Foods

Your Go-To Grocery Guide for a Mediterranean Pantry

1. **Fruits:**

   - Berries (blueberries, strawberries, raspberries)

   - Cherries

   - Oranges

   - Pineapple

   - Papaya

   - Apples

   - Pears

   - Kiwi

- Watermelon

- Mango

2. **Vegetables:**

   - Leafy greens (spinach, kale, Swiss chard)

   - Broccoli

   - Cauliflower

   - Brussels sprouts

   - Bell peppers

   - Carrots

   - Sweet potatoes

   - Tomatoes

   - Cabbage

   - Zucchini

3. **Whole Grains:**

   - Quinoa

   - Brown rice

- Oats

- Whole wheat

- Barley

- Buckwheat

- Farro

4. **Legumes:**

   - Lentils

   - Chickpeas (garbanzo beans)

   - Black beans

   - Kidney beans

   - Pinto beans

5. **Nuts and Seeds:**

   - Almonds

   - Walnuts

   - Flaxseeds

   - Chia seeds

- Hemp seeds

6. **Healthy Fats:**

   - Extra virgin olive oil

   - Avocado

   - Fatty fish (salmon, mackerel, sardines)

   - Walnuts

   - Chia seeds

7. **Herbs and Spices:**

   - Turmeric

   - Ginger

   - Garlic

   - Cinnamon

   - Rosemary

   - Thyme

   - Oregano

   - Basil

8. **Beverages:**

   - Green tea

   - Herbal teas (chamomile, ginger, turmeric)

   - Water infused with citrus fruits and herbs

9. **Dairy and Dairy Alternatives:**

   - Greek yogurt

   - Kefir

   - Almond milk (unsweetened)

10. **Lean Proteins:**

    - Skinless poultry (chicken, turkey)

    - Lean cuts of grass-fed beef

    - Eggs

    - Plant-based protein sources (tofu, tempeh)

11. **Dark Chocolate:**

    - Choose chocolate with a high cocoa content (70% or higher)

12. Others:

- Honey (raw, unprocessed)

- Red onions

- Mushrooms

4-WEEK

MEAL
PLANNER

S M T W T F S

○ ○ ○ ○ ○ ○ ○

Meals

Special Meal

breakfast:

lunch:

dinner:

Shopping List

- ----------------------- TO BUY
- -----------------------
- -----------------------
- -----------------------
- -----------------------
- -----------------------

To do list

Notes and Tips

TO DO

S M T W T F S

○ ○ ○ ○ ○ ○ ○

Meals

breakfast:

lunch:

dinner:

Special Meal

Shopping List

TO BUY

- --------------------------------
- --------------------------------
- --------------------------------
- --------------------------------
- --------------------------------
- --------------------------------

To do list

Notes and Tips

TO DO

S M T W T F S

Meals

breakfast:

lunch:

dinner:

Special Meal

To do list

Shopping List

- ----------------------------- TO BUY
- -----------------------------
- -----------------------------
- -----------------------------
- -----------------------------

Notes and Tips

_____
_____
_____
_____

TO DO

S M T W T F S

○ ○ ○ ○ ○ ○ ○

Meals

breakfast:

lunch:

dinner:

Special Meal

Shopping List

- ---------------------
- --------------------- TO BUY
- ---------------------
- ---------------------
- ---------------------
- ---------------------

To do list

Notes and Tips

TO DO

S M T W T F S
○ ○ ○ ○ ○ ○ ○

Meals

Special Meal

breakfast:

lunch:

dinner:

Shopping List

- ------------------------------ TO BU:
- ------------------------------
- ------------------------------
- ------------------------------
- ------------------------------
- ------------------------------

To do list

Notes and Tips

_____
_____
_____
_____

S M T W T F S

Meals

breakfast:

lunch:

dinner:

Special Meal

Shopping List

- ----------------------
- ---------------------- TO BUY
- ----------------------
- ----------------------
- ----------------------
- ----------------------

To do list

Notes and Tips

TO DO

S M T W T F S

Meals

breakfast:

lunch:

dinner:

Special Meal

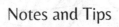

Shopping List

TO BUY

- ----------------------------
- ----------------------------
- ----------------------------
- ----------------------------
- ----------------------------
- ----------------------------

To do list

Notes and Tips

TO DO

S M T W T F S

Meals

breakfast:

lunch:

dinner:

Special Meal

Shopping List

- ----------------------
- ---------------------- **TO BUY**
- ----------------------
- ----------------------
- ----------------------
- ----------------------

To do list

Notes and Tips

TO DO

S M T W T F S

Meals

breakfast:

lunch:

dinner:

Special Meal

Shopping List

- ------------------------
- ------------------------
- ------------------------
- ------------------------
- ------------------------
- ------------------------

TO BUY

To do list

Notes and Tips

TO DO

S M T W T F S

○ ○ ○ ○ ○ ○ ○

Meals

breakfast:

lunch:

dinner:

Special Meal

To do list

Shopping List

- ---------------------- 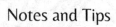 TO BUY
- ----------------------
- ----------------------------
- ----------------------
- ----------------------
- ----------------------

Notes and Tips

_____
_____
_____
_____

TO DO

S M T W T F S

○ ○ ○ ○ ○ ○ ○

Meals

breakfast:

lunch:

dinner:

Special Meal

To do list

Shopping List

● ----------------------------- TO BU
● -----------------------------
● -----------------------------
● -----------------------------
● -----------------------------
● -----------------------------

Notes and Tips

_____
_____
_____
_____

TO DO

S M T W T F S

Meals

breakfast:

lunch:

dinner:

Special Meal

Shopping List

- ----------------------
- ---------------------- TO BUY
- ----------------------------
- --------------------------
- ------------------------
- ------------------------

To do list

Notes and Tips

_____
_____
_____
_____

TO DO

S   M   T   W   T   F   S

Meals

breakfast:

lunch:

dinner:

Special Meal

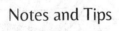

Shopping List

TO BUY

- --------------------------------
- --------------------------------
- --------------------------------
- --------------------------------
- --------------------------------
- --------------------------------

To do list

Notes and Tips

TO DO

S M T W T F S

Meals

breakfast:

lunch:

dinner:

Special Meal

Shopping List

- ------------------------ TO BUY
- ------------------------
- ------------------------
- ------------------------
- ------------------------
- ------------------------

To do list

Notes and Tips

TO DO

S M T W T F S

Meals

breakfast:

lunch:

dinner:

Special Meal

Shopping List

- ---------------------- TO BUY
- ----------------------
- ----------------------
- ----------------------
- ----------------------
- ----------------------

To do list

Notes and Tips

TO DO

S M T W T F S

○ ○ ○ ○ ○ ○ ○

Meals

breakfast:

lunch:

dinner:

Special Meal

Shopping List

- ------------------------ **TO BUY**
- ------------------------
- ------------------------
- ------------------------
- ------------------------
- ------------------------

To do list

Notes and Tips

TO DO

S M T W T F S

○ ○ ○ ○ ○ ○ ○

Meals

Special Meal

breakfast:

lunch:

dinner:

Shopping List

● ------------------------
● ------------------------
● ------------------------
● ------------------------
● ------------------------
● ------------------------

TO BU

To do list

Notes and Tips

TO DO

S M T W T F S

Meals

breakfast:

lunch:

dinner:

Special Meal

To do list

Shopping List

● ------------------------------ TO BUY
● ------------------------------
● ------------------------------
● ------------------------------
● ------------------------------
● ------------------------------

Notes and Tips

TO DO

S M T W T F S

Meals

breakfast:

lunch:

dinner:

Special Meal

Shopping List

- ----------------------
- ---------------------- 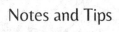 TO BUY
- ----------------------
- ----------------------
- ----------------------
- ----------------------

To do list

Notes and Tips

TO DO

S	M	T	W	T	F	S
○	○	○	○	○	○	○

Meals

breakfast:

lunch:

dinner:

Special Meal

To do list

Shopping List

- ---------------------- TO BUY
- ----------------------
- ----------------------
- ----------------------
- ----------------------
- ----------------------

Notes and Tips

TO DO

S M T W T F S

○ ○ ○ ○ ○ ○ ○

Meals

breakfast:

lunch:

dinner:

Special Meal

To do list

Shopping List

● ----------------------------
● ---------------------------- **TO BUY**
● ----------------------------
● ----------------------------
● ----------------------------
● ----------------------------

Notes and Tips

TO DO

S M T W T F S

Meals

breakfast:

lunch:

dinner:

Special Meal

To do list

Shopping List

- --------------------------
- --------------------- **TO BUY**
- --------------------------
- ----------------------
- ----------------------
- ----------------------

Notes and Tips

_____
_____
_____
_____

TO DO

S M T W T F S

Meals

breakfast:

lunch:

dinner:

Special Meal

To do list

Shopping List

- ------------------------ TO BU
- ------------------------
- ------------------------------
- ------------------------------
- ------------------------------
- ------------------------------

Notes and Tips

_____
_____
_____
_____

TO DO

S M T W T F S

Meals

breakfast:

lunch:

dinner:

Special Meal

Shopping List

- --------------------- **TO BUY**
- ---------------------
- -----------------------
- -----------------------
- -----------------------
- -----------------------

To do list

Notes and Tips

TO DO

S M T W T F S

Meals

breakfast:

lunch:

dinner:

Special Meal

Shopping List

● ------------------------
● ------------------------ TO BUY
● ------------------------
● ------------------------
● ------------------------
● ------------------------

To do list

Notes and Tips

TO DO

S M T W T F S
○ ○ ○ ○ ○ ○ ○

Meals

breakfast:

lunch:

dinner:

Special Meal

Shopping List

- -------------------------
- ------------------------- TO BUY
- -------------------------
- -------------------------
- -------------------------
- -------------------------

To do list

Notes and Tips

TO DO

S M T W T F S

Meals

breakfast:

lunch:

dinner:

Special Meal

Shopping List

- _____
- _____ TO BUY
- _____
- _____
- _____
- _____

To do list

_____
_____
_____
_____
_____
_____

Notes and Tips

TO DO

S M T W T F S

○ ○ ○ ○ ○ ○ ○

Meals

breakfast:

lunch:

dinner:

Special Meal

Shopping List

- ----------------------
- ---------------------- TO BUY
- ----------------------
- ----------------------
- ----------------------
- ----------------------

To do list

Notes and Tips

TO DO

Made in the USA
Las Vegas, NV
27 October 2024

10541340R00089